The Grizedale Experience

The Grizedale Experience

Sculpture, Arts & Theatre in a Lakeland Forest

Editors

Bill Grant & Paul Harris

A PAUL HARRIS BOOK
For Canongate Press

First Published 1991 by
Canongate Press
14 Frederick Street
Edinburgh
EH2 2HB

ISBN 0 86241 349 4 Cased
ISBN 0 86241 354 0 Paperback

Production by Paul Harris Editorial, Whittingehame House, Haddington, EH41 4QA. Typeset in Scotland by Falcon Typographic Ltd, Edinburgh and London, and printed in Yugoslavia by Gorenjski Tisk, Kranj.

LOCATION MAP

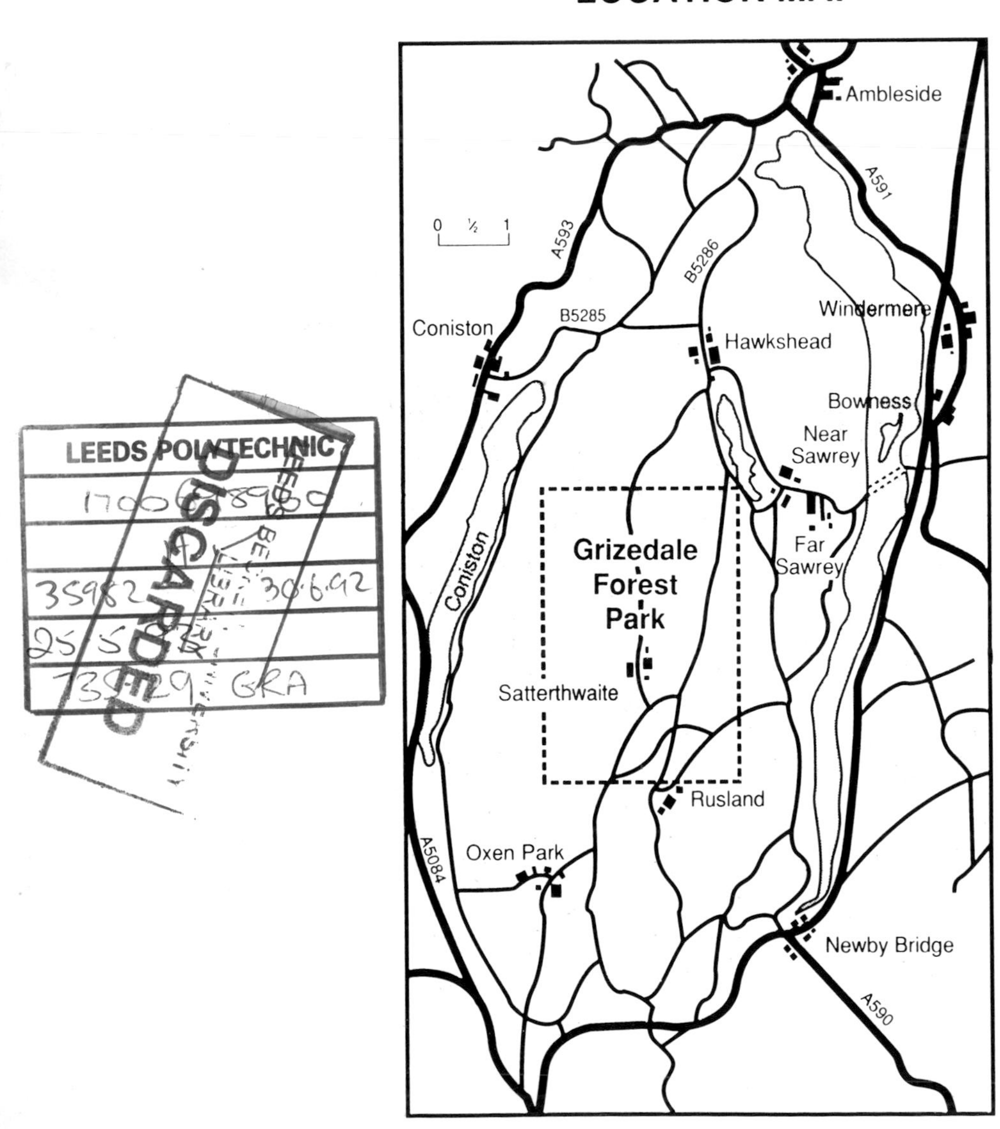

Contents

taken place involving students and graduates, bird watchers, fishery experts, biologists, archaeologists and schoolchildren. They discover a wealth of information about Grizedale which otherwise would never have been studied. Young students of widely differing disciplines are finding opportunities to bring their studies into the countryside and, simultaneously, make a contribution towards a better understanding of the forest ecosystem.

Travels in the New World, thanks to a Winston Churchill Travelling Fellowship to the U.S.A. and Canada in 1968, not only confirmed my views that quality was the most important factor in the provision of recreational facilities, it also spawned the concept of the Theatre in the Forest. A day time forest experience followed by a cultural experience in the evening fired my imagination. However, when I put the idea to a working committee, cries of derision greeted me, the very thought of such a radical proposal. How would people get there? Theatres were in towns! What about the winters? How would it be financed? Who would run it? How ridiculous to think that artists would come to such an unlikely venue they said. But when I put the idea to Alex Schouvallof, the Director of the North West Arts Association, it was greeted with enthusiasm: "I can't fund you," he said, "but the vision is wonderful. Have a go and we will help with programme suggestions." I thanked him for his confidence and the Grizedale Society was born. The voluntary committee were hand picked, not for their knowledge of the arts, but for their particular skills!

We negotiated the legal structure with Rowland Hart Jackson our solicitor, who dealt with the Constitution for the Charity Commissioners to obtain charitable status and, bless him, he never sent an account for his invaluable advice and services. The negotiation of the lease of the building with the Forestry Commission was complicated. To agree "heads of terms" for a lease was no easy task. The Forestry Commission had nothing in their terms of remit to allow theatres to operate within their property! Government departments have standard leases which, of course, didn't accord with how we wished to work. Clauses were inserted, altered, deleted, redrafted, argued over and the files grew fat with correspondence but, eventually, a satisfactory compromise was reached. Meanwhile, we laboured evenings and weekends and we built the stage, then a bar. More than two decades later, Norman Howgate still runs the bar he built! We raised the beams, built the raking, and manufactured the seats with timber from the forest.

In the hay loft above the coach yard, underneath the grime and dirt of fifty years, we found a rather nice hall. It is to the credit of this working voluntary committee that the project has prospered. Meanwhile, with the minimum of basic lighting, four spotlights and two floods, we started to programme the Theatre. We turned again to the Director of North Western Arts Association. He suggested some artists, put us in touch with some agents. It was sufficient to get us on the way and, thereafter, we learned the hard way. The decision to structure the programme to cover as wide a spectrum of events as possible was deliberate. This broad programme of promotions ensured that we attracted the maximum range of audience involvement, a policy which has continued ever since. We aimed for artistic quality and diversity to build up confidence with our patrons, and the policy has paid dividends, artistically, with consistently high audience support.

With the Performing Arts established and on a very sound administrative base, opportunities to move forward to further initiatives were

Bill Grant in The Theatre in the Forest. Photograph by Terry Bromley

possible. With the minimum of administration costs and a high level of artistic performance we were able to travel fast because we travelled light. This developed an independence of thought and action and financial acumen.

In 1974 the reorganisation of county boundaries brought us out of North West Arts Association and into Northern Arts. This was an important move from our point of view and we formed a much closer liaison with our Regional Arts Association than ever before.

At Northern Arts' suggestion we moved into the Visual Arts, and 1977 saw the establishment of the Grizedale Sculpture Project. Here, our administrative experience proved vital. This more neglected art form required special support. Sited against the dramatic back cloth of a large working forest give the sculptures (site specific) character and mysticism. The Society in this field has always performed a catalyst role: bringing the forest environment and the artists together; providing the servicing and support and allowing the sculptors to respond to the situation; encouraging innovation, creativity and diversity. The project has now achieved a national profile, and the use of artists from Europe, Asia and the U.S.A. has given an international focus. Many young sculptors have become established at Grizedale and have repaid our investment in full.

The experience of being in a small local community, and with the challenge of a nine thousand acre forest, with around sixty works already *in situ*, has the effect of stretching and releasing young sculptors from previous inhibitions and working methods. A residency at Grizedale sends them away quite different people and so more "complete" artists.

In 1988, we leased the redundant Saw Mill at Grizedale for a peppercorn rent. This building, earmarked for demolition, to provide another ten car park spaces, was only saved at the last moment. Converted into the Gallery in the Forest it now houses a didactic exhibition, giving back up and leading people into a greater appreciation of sculpture and in the open air. The conversion costs came from money raised by our own efforts from Trusts and Foundations, and with a grant from the Rural Development Commission.

The Gallery opened up further expansion projects. Whilst converting it the opportunity was taken to upgrade a delapidated "lean to" which adjoined the mill. At a stroke, an existing eyesore was removed, and a workshop created for craft workers. Equipped with wood working machinery, thanks to a grant from the Crafts Council, the society now offers residencies for crafts people, working mainly with wood.

More recently, the large attic space above the gallery has been transformed into a studio for painters – who knows what this exciting and creative space may produce?

The Grizedale Society has grown organically, developing a down to earth approach to Art. Whilst it does not slot easily into the "established Arts scene", the blend of voluntary and professional expertise has achieved consistently high artistic performance.

Above all, it has remained faithful to its concept of quality, without pretentiousness. The pleasure and fulfilment it has brought to our patrons and artists alike is a real reward.

At Grizedale, the Society has fused the arts and nature into a complete experience in the environs of this working forest. In this rural situation the Society has offered opportunities to actors, musicians, sculptors, painters, crafts people, poets, writers, teachers and natural historians, which, in turn, has helped regenerate the economy of the community.

The "role model" position which the Society so effectively demonstrates has influenced and stimulated a new awareness of the importance of the Arts to the quality of life in rural areas.

The Grizedale Experience must surely signal how much can be achieved when a number of ogranisations work in concord, each contributing to the whole. At Grizedale, Northern Arts supports the Society with core funding and expertise, the Forestry Commission provides the space and accommodation buildings at an economic rent whilst the Grizedale Society contributes the flair, the imagination and above all, the courage to bring the vision to fruition.

Bill Grant

The Grizedale Experience

If this story were simply about landmarks in history, like so many notches on a stick, it would begin when Norsemen settled in "Pig-valley" (or "Grize-Dale"), in the 9th century AD. For it was then that great tracts of virgin forest were cleared to make way for agriculture. Later, the effects of charcoal burning, iron smelting and the timber industry, would leave only 1200 acres of woodland from a forest that once covered the entire Furness peninsula between Lake Windermere and Coniston Water.

If this were an account of afforestation of the area, it would not begin until 1936, the year the Forestry Commission first acquired the Grizedale Estate from Harold Brocklebank – the Liverpool ship owner and Cunard tycoon.

For those who see Grizedale as the most important collection of site-specific sculpture in Europe, the story dates from the commissioning of the first sculptor-in-residence in 1977.

But to really tell the story which embraces all that Grizedale represents and all that it has achieved, we have to go back . . . 400 million years.

Spend an hour in one of Europe's grandest galleries and your feet begin to ache, tiredness creeps through your body and you start to wonder where all the air went. After two hours you feel like nudging one of the attendants from his chair just to sit down for five minutes – or so it seems at the time.

For artists and art-audiences everywhere, Grizedale is a breath of fresh air. A place to spend a day, a week or several months at a time. For it takes time. Time to roam the forests and time to visit the arts-centre, time to think and time to learn.

When the Forestry Commission acquired the Estate it consisted of 3,500 acres of rough grazing and woodland, together with the village of Satterthwaite, Grizedale Hall with its policy woodlands and its associated outbuildings. It is the renovated outbuildings and mews which now form the Grizedale centre.

The history of large, though not necessarily "grand" buildings, consists of the history of the people that stayed in them. Sadly, after the war, occupancy of Grizedale Hall became increasingly rare. Prior to demolition in 1957 the hall's claim to fame was as a POW camp which had provided room-service for the likes of Rudolph Hess. All that remains is the former terrace and ornamental stone gates of the West entrance.

On the other hand, the neighbouring village of Satterthwaite has remained relatively unchanged. The school, founded in 1848, is still a school. Some of the slate-built period houses offer Bed and Breakfast and a sensitive policy of barn-conversion and housing in-fill has steered the village clear of exploitation. The Post Office and the pub are perhaps the only places where tourists stop and linger. If there were a collective name for this sort of gathering, given the local climate, it would be a "Kagool of tourists". But it is the Forestry Commission – not tourism – that is the major employer.

The main concern for The Forestry Commission lay with the land. Afforestation began in 1936 and continued throughout the war. The most important aims were to begin planned timber production which would also re-establish a whole range of habitats for wild animals and birds.

Grizedale Hall, demolished 1957.

The Commission were well aware of the unique features at Grizedale. In particular as home to the only indigenous herd of red deer in England, to have lived entirely in woodland.

The innovative thinking that would lift the reputation of Grizedale from a well-managed acreage of forest to an internationally known centre for the arts, would not come until later. For this to happen, an irresistible current of new ideas would need to flow through the steadfast methods of foresters. The flow started in 1963, with the arrival of Bill Grant and a policy that gave the public access to Commission land.

Bill Grant joined the Forestry Commission in 1936. After war-service in the Far East, he returned to work in Thornthwaite Forest, then at Greystoke, also in Cumbria. He came to Grizedale with his wife Elsie who had been brought up in Cumberland. But it was for his deep-rooted knowledge and love of wild-life that he was appointed as Head Forester.

Small lakes were introduced into the forest, attracting mallards, teal and greylags. The pine-marten returned, and the reintroduction of the capercaillie, not recorded since the seventeenth century was attempted. With the flourishing habitats came the predators, and the golden eagle can once more be seen soaring above the forests of Furness.

Bill Grant and his staff put into practice a fully integrated recreational plan incorporating nature trails, forest walks, wild-life observation towers – positively encouraging such outdoor pursuits as orienteering, fishing and deer-stalking.

The deer museum, set up in 1956 to instruct forest workers in the principles and techniques of selective deer control, was expanded into a wild life centre in its own right. A place where the public could come and learn about the forest community and take away a helpful brochure for their friends.

Large numbers of visitors now had to be accommodated within a forest that had only recently managed to balance ecological aims with those of timber production. Areas were set aside for tourists, with car parks, camp-sites, and forest walks. Naturalists aiming to study particular habitats were directed to deeper parts of the forest, and restricted zones were set aside for long term research projects concerned with wild life management.

The enormous success of the recreational plan within a thriving forest environment attracted professional, political and media interest, and in 1968 Bill Grant was awarded a Winston Churchill Travelling Fellowship to North America.

Upon his return it was obvious that the original flow of ideas merely formed a springboard from which exciting and radical artistic ventures were to be launched: The Theatre in the Forest, The Visitors Centre, The Gallery, The Craft Studios, and the unique sculpture project located along a ten-mile ramble known as The Silurian Way.

In 1977, The Grizedale Society commissioned Richard Harris as the first sculptor in residence – to conceive and create a sculpture using natural materials found in the forest. The idea of having site-specific sculpture in a forest environment was encouraged by Northern Arts who still fund the residency scheme today.

There are currently more than 60 sculptures situated throughout the forest and many of the artists have been brought to prominence as a direct result of their work at Grizedale. Andy Goldsworthy, David Kemp, Richard Harris and Andy Frost are some of the more familiar names, but artists have come from as far afield as the United States and Japan.

The attractions are obvious: a chance to work in the peace and quiet of an English Forest, to use nature as a guide, to deal with woodland materials, textures and shapes. To become captivated by the magical qualities of the forest.

For the rambler the result is no less astounding, because site-specific sculpture is non-intrusive and serves to heighten an appreciation of its setting. The forest – a wild work of art that has taken nature millenia to perfect – is suddenly explainable. Wandering through the forest thus enlightened, Pantheistic thoughts begin to surface. It is creative and satisfying to artist and visitor alike.

The Silurian Way which opened in 1973, retains that all important element of discovery. Some works degrade very quickly, others made

Bill Grant with the prestigious Prudential awards

from the bronze-grey, Silurian slate suggest they have been there since time began. The slate is some 400 million years old, and its use in sculpture in the forest, has meant the geology of the area itself, plays an integral part in the Grizedale story.

Its a story involving hundreds of thousands of visitors annually. A story of the vision and courage of the Forestry Commission; of the continued goodwill and understanding of the local community, and the co-operation and support from a number of arts organisations throughout Britain. It's a story involving hundreds of professional artists, from those performing in the forest theatre, to those taking up residencies in local schools.

But, above all, The Grizedale centre and all that it offers, owes much of its existence to the energy and enthusiasm of Bill Grant. "If we have achieved anything, it has been to prove that the arts are not the prerogative of towns and cities, but play an important role in the rural environment based upon creativity, excellence, diversity, and above all accessibility. This is satisfaction enough."

Iain McLean

The Theatre in the Forest

In 1968 Bill Grant, chief forester at Grizedale, was awarded a Winston Churchill Travelling Fellowship to North America. His brief was to study the "Educational Aspects of Wildlife Conservation", and his visit was to have a profound effect on his future thinking back home in Grizedale.

The most influential discovery was the number of small theatres within many of the National Parks and forests. Their purpose was to entertain and educate the public on aspects of conservation and the husbanding of natural resources. On his return, Bill talked with conservator Jack Chard who gave full support to the exciting and innovative proposal to start a similar venture at Grizedale. From then on, the desire for a Theatre in the Forest would not diminish.

Small-scale presentations were held in the grain store in the old coach yard. Here, guests would present lectures on the flora and fauna of the forest, show photographic slides of wildlife and hold poetry readings. It was a good start, though it was hardly the Theatre that Bill had envisaged. That required money. But where to go for funding?

A year into the project, and a televised documentary screened moves to bring the arts to remote areas of the country. Encouraged by the programme, Bill sought contact with North West Arts, who together with representatives from the Arts Council came to the forest to see for themselves.

A number of other funding bodies were to follow and, impressed by Bill's vision for a theatre at Grizedale, it became possible to realise the cost of converting the theatre through grants from The English Tourist Board and The Guilbenkian foundation. But the greatest contribution of all – people – was still to come.

The Grizedale Society was set up in 1969 and registered as a charitable trust the following year. Understanding the enormity of the project, Bill Grant set up a working committee whose members included, the assistant director of a local museum, a builder, a painter, two carpenters and several part-time bar-staff. From this core group, the whole venture was launched on a tide of enthusiasm.

The building chosen for conversion was a coach-house with a high hay loft. Built at the turn of the century, its structure sound, renovation work could begin immediately on the interior. Beneath half a century of grime they found an attractive wood floor. The voluntary committee, set to: sanding the floor, sealing the walls and restoring the dark, heavy roof beams.

The carpenters organised the construction of bench seating from Grizedale forest timber. Electricians were contracted to install the complex lighting system required for a purpose-designed theatre. Central heating was installed. In total the project was completed for £25,000. It was really remarkably little for a theatre with a 230-seat auditorium, a 31 x 23 foot stage, and a comfortable bar-reception area. Even so, grants didn't cover everything and the Theatre had to be a paying concern from the opening night.

One night in May 1970, The Northern Dance Company played to a packed house. It was, unfortunately, soon apparent that only the first couple of rows could see the dancers feet. Somewhat naively for a theatre design, the seating had been constructed on one level.

Watercolour by Colin Whittle: *Recital in The Theatre in the Forest.* The event depicted is a piano recital by John Lill, July 1986

Raked seating was the only solution, and the whole lot had to be dismantled and re-designed. The extra timber needed for beams was donated by Lord Lonsdale, a local landowner, and the volunteers set to – seven nights a week, for two months. Finally, Grizedale had its Theatre in the Forest and the acoustics turned out to be excellent. A year later, the Theatre was awarded a "Come to Britain" trophy for outstanding tourist enterprise.

The Grizedale Theatre in the Forest exists to provide quality entertainment in as many forms as possible. Something for everybody: from opera, piano and violin recitals to jazz and folk nights. From drama to dance.

On still summer nights, the sound of applause emanates from this multi-purpose theatre, like a wind rippling through the leaves of the surrounding forest. Applause to over fifteen hundred events since its inception.

Classical musicians such as John Lill, Julian Lloyd Webber, André Tchaikovsky and Amadeus Quartet have all been well received. Grizedale now boasts its own annual piano festival and the popular "Classics on Sunday" series of recitals.

Ballet Rambert and Moving Visions Dance Theatre have performed here. From the jazz world: Kenny Ball, George Chisholm, Chris Barber, Humphrey Lyttelton and George Melly. Folk music is also popularly represented with concerts by Jimmy McGregor, Julie Felix, The Corries and the MacCalmans.

Variety made its debut with performances by Richard Stilgoe, Cyril Fletcher, Donald Swann and others. Ken Dodd first saw the Theatre in a TV documentary and immediately phoned his agent to get a booking for his one-man show. He recalls: "Driving up there at night, I felt as if I was in the middle of *A Midsummer Night's Dream*. I might joke about it being a hut in a wood but it is one of the best Theatres I've ever played. The wonderfully intimate atmosphere is quite unique".

Grizedale is special. It will always draw great stage artists. People dedicated to the thrill of live performance, to the survival of British Theatre – in every neck of the woods.

"I simply wrote to Dame Flora Robson," Bill Grant recalls, "and told her we'd got this little theatre in the middle of nowhere, and she agreed to come".

As have others: Antony Hopkins, Dame Judi Dench and Geraldine McEwen in plays ranging from Shakespeare's *The Taming of the Shrew*, to Willy Russell's modern classic *Educating Rita*.

Yet ironically, apart from a relatively small annual grant from Northern Arts, all the income derives from box-office returns. As houses tend to average around 80 percent the Theatre continues to thrive two decades later.

The Grizedale Society has around one thousand members. Regular patrons who remember the exciting times within the years of hard work. Such as the time they had to raise over two thousand pounds to salvage one of the last Steinway pianos built in Hamburg. Naturally, they achieved their target – for what better piano to lure the best exponents of the art into a remote forest location?

Even today that same dedication and determination is ever-present. The Theatre is run on a voluntary basis by members who man the box-office, sell programmes, and stand on the door.

Grizedale Theatre in the Forest exists in the traditions of the earliest arenas – as a place of spectacle. Where the talented can come and perform, where the audience can come and marvel, for no other reason than to enjoy themselves. And any wind rippling through the forest leaves, is quite happy to accommodate and applaud them.

As Bill says, "I believe in quality. If you've got the quality right then other things slot into place."

Iain McLean

Performance in the theatre, 1989: Caroline Dale (cello) and the Thaxted String Trio

Grizedale Forest Sculpture

The Sculpture Project was initiated in 1977 to enable sculptures to work in a forest. At that time there was not much evidence of art in the landscape and, for that matter, public art commission was not very evident in the U.K. Questioning was also taking place about the most appropriate and effective way state monies could be channelled for the patronage of the individual artist. The North American experience through the Works Programme Administration (W.P.A.), which made payment to artists for professional services in the community, was much admired. The concern was a shift from the notion of artists support to offer of opportunity. The aim was to establish a unique situation for the artist, the host venue and the public. Grizedale in its early days was centred upon the experience for the individual, and it was later that the public was addressed.

Grizedale is based on artists' residences which last up to six months. The vitality of the project springs from the sculptor's response to the working forest and the questions it poses for his or her sculptural practice. Some sculpture is of a temporary nature whilst other work is more permanent. A refreshing diversity in approach is shown in the sculpture, which is reflected in the subject matter and the working methods. Sympathetic to the forest landscape, the sculptures are all sited by the sculptors.

Where does Grizedale stand in relation to other contemporary visual arts positions and perspectives? In one sense Grizedale is difficult to locate. One can tick off what it is not. It is not a Sculpture Park, not just a permanent collection of sited works. It is not a temporary exhibition venue. It is not driven by the ambitions of the newly arrived Public Art Agencies or the market economy of Percent for Art. It is not about the opportunities offered by land reclamation, nor is Grizedale a country cousin of the National Garden Festivals. Yet compared to Grizedale the installations and performance, even platform, created by organisations such as Edge appear to be of an urban order. As one might expect there is a natural affinity with environmental and green campaigning (art) groups, most notably Common Ground, but their central concern is of a different nature. However, what helps make Grizedale such a rich experience is that threads from those various issues can be seen in the project.

Grizedale is most often compared to an Artist Symposia which are most associated with Eastern Europe. Artists are gathered together in one place to work over a set period of time often using a material or responding to a particular situation. Again, however, the structuring and concerns are different. Grizedale artists have a common experience which comes primarily from an individual response to place. The artist is given time to work, and to respond to the space. Grizedale has similarly not been about a community art approach. The central mission is about the artist living and working in a small rural community. Grizedale celebrates an individual's response to a particular landscape, a large production forest.

The English landscape is a history of land, estate and power. The Cistercian monks of Furness Abbey enclosed the fells for sheep farming. The dry stone walls are useful material for the contemporary sculptor! The coppice woods were used for fuel for heating, for charcoal burning, iron smelting and potash making. Domestic and agricultural buildings and implements were made from what was on hand. Many of the processes used in making functional objects are being re-explored by the late 20th century craftsworker. The first sculptor's studio was in an old water powered mill.

In 1937 the estate of Harold Brocklebank of Cunard Line fame was acquired by the Forestry Commission and the Grizedale Fells were planted. In the Second World War Grizedale Hall served as a German Officer's Prisoner of War Camp. *The Plague Dog*, the title of a sculpture by Kevin Harrison refers to the Plague Dogs in Richard Adams book of that name. The historical, social, and cultural backcloth of Grizedale intervenes with landscape; nowhere is it neutral. The human presence in the land is ever evident; from the Stone Circles at Swinside, to the formal gardens at Levens Hall, from the hill sheep farms, to the rail and the motorways, from Sellafield on the West coast and to the Lake District's tourist facilities. Carl André has described England as one large earthwork. The economic use of land has clothed the form of the land. What is presently being explored is the space (mental, physical, and economic) that this condition has created for artists.

There is an awareness of the growing conditions, seasons and climate for English sculpture. For Henry Moore "Sculpture is an art of the open air daylight. Sunlight is necessary to it and for me it's best setting and complement is nature. I would rather have a piece of my sculpture in a landscape, almost any landscape than in or at the most beautiful building I know." The isolated stone circles of Castlerigg, Long Meg and Her Daughters and Swinside sited in the Cumbrian fells engender a sense of place. Richard Long, who has not worked at Grizedale, in many ways underlines the approach and sensibility. "These works are made of the

place, they are a rearrangement of it and in time will be re-absorbed by it. I hope to make work for the land not against it."

Henry Moore has always been "there", so monumental that in a sense he created space and freedom for later generations of sculptors. Over the Lake District, though, it is the presence of William Wordsworth that holds sway. "Nothing conveys an idea of beauty more strongly than the Lake; nor of horror than the mountains; and the former lying in the lap of the latter, expresses in a strong manner the mode of their combination. Thus William Gilpin in *Observations on the Mountains and Lakes of Cumberland and Westmorland* helped to popularise the "picturesque". The presences of nature were to compel the imagination of 19th Century. Around Wordsworth were grouped poets and prose writers who helped change the way the Lake District was perceived. A generation later, John Ruskin moved to Brantwood by Coniston Water, the estates of which back onto Grizedale Forest. Kurt Schwitters, after moving to Ambleside in 1945, began his third Merzbau at Clyinders in the nearby Langdale Valley. So we come to the present Grizedale Forest sculptors who are exploring issues relating to the place of art and the artist in the landscape.

The early sculptors had a more difficult time of it, but as the project became more accepted by the conservative rural community it became progressively easier for each "new" sculptor. There was an art base to play against. Lessons were learnt. Sculptors seldom have the opportunity to site work and to consider scale related to a forest environment. Grizedale in some respects is a large public studio, with few restrictions and no necessary planning legislation.

All the sculptors accept the impermanence of their work. This is highlighted by David Kemp's proposal to see *Scale Green Birdman* fall into "aesthetic" decay. It will be interesting to see in the future how

Gligor Stefanov – Yugoslavia
Cherubic Wings 1990

"Cherubic wings are spread in Grizedale Forest. The timbers were installed where they had been felled by savage storms, the branches, fixed with glue, expressing tense rhythm. The dynamics and geometrical shapes of the wings are clearly demonstrative of a moment in time when they were locked in a battle with the savage gales which brought them down."

work with the environment using the materials and conditions that the Forest naturally has to offer."

Similarly Richard Harris made his sculpture from the materials of the forest. "Stone is fundamental to my work; in the forest rock is never far from the surface, breaking through in craggy outcrops. I collect slate from old drystone walls which run through the forest left over from an old field system." Silurian slate is hard acid rock which is difficult to carve. Steel has been seldom used, but it is not entirely foreign as the ironmasters relentlessly cut the forests to convert timber into charcoal for smelting the Furness iron ore.

David Kemp initially had a problem looking for Cornish scrap in a Lake District forest – "the embryo of the idea is already in it." Andy Goldsworthy, faced with coming to terms with the pine forest, used the "material" to force himself to think and work in new ways. "In this respect I have always felt a massive potential at Grizedale to provoke change . . . not only to make me see things afresh but provide means by which I was able to draw together experiences, forms and ideas from work in other places and materials – ice, bracken, sticks, mud, stones, etc."

"Through the startled deer and the squeaks and screech of birds and buzzards wheeling in the thermals" the artists are very conscious of their wild life companions. Satterthwaite and Grizedale are derived from Norse meaning "Summer clearing" and "valley of the pigs". Wild swine roamed the Forest in medieval times. The red deer of the Furness Fells are the only true indigenous herd in Britain and records go back some 600 years. There is also a good population of roe deer. *The Realm of Taurus* by Keir Smith was concerned "with animals as an economic resource (from hunting and trapping of wild creatures to animal husbandry)." The spider, lizard, hedgehog, deer, boar, sheep, rabbit, heron, ducks and rooks have all inspired work. There is Sally Matthew's narrative tableau of lurcher dogs hunting a pregnant hind. Even David Nash's *Running Table* has an animal quality.

Such time in the Forest celebrates a "sharpening" of the senses, the awareness of the "wind, night, and darkness and all changes of weather. David Nash "was gently drawn into the metabolism, pace and energy of the Forest." Ken Turnell makes a more pointed remark, "the wettest summer I have known." Grizedale has a mild oceanic climate, with some 75 inches of rain a year. Rain falls two days in every three. Gales, referred to by the foresters as the "great harvester", can blow down large areas of forest. Windblown timber is useful for sculptors!

Few artists have undertaken the challenge of siting work in the conifer plantations. The upward energy of the Sitka and Norway Spruce, the Japanese and European larch though does appear to have references to church architecture, particularly the cathedral. *Forest Fugue*, for instance, stands at the end of a long nave. The organ is playing a silent requiem for the cut trees. Again this feeling is echoed in Andy Goldworthy's *Seven Spires* which has "a similarity in the subdued brown light and stillness found in both cathedrals and pine forests." More recently Richard Harris' *Hollow Spruce*, a mysterious wave in the deep forest, has opened up new possibilities.

The Grizedale Experience has influenced a generation of sculptors and art administrators particularly as it relates to public art and artist patronage schemes. There is now more support for siting work in the outdoor urban environment through the interests of architects, planners, and landscape architects. More sympathy is evident towards the purchase of artists time towards a specific commission rather than an off the-shelf studio purchase. The international attention directed at the project, and its belief in supporting young unknown artists, is a good base for moving forward.

The Grizedale Society's Sculpture Project offers a unique opportunity to both the artist and the public to explore and experience. It has created a higher artist profile and helped open up discussions with various public(s) and professions. If some measure of their aims and ambitions are achieved it will signal a proper role for the visual arts, crafts and performing arts in a rural community as we approach the millennium. It is essentially a role based on the artist working in the landscape.

Peter Davies
Visual Arts Officer
Northern Arts

Andy Goldsworthy
The Wall that went for a Walk 1990

"We started in February deliberately so we would be there coming out of winter into Spring, the days becoming progressively longer and warmer.

The trees came into leaf, first the larch, then the willows and and hazels and the oaks last. I was gently drawn into the metabolism, pace and energy of the forest."

David Nash
Running Table 1978

"Realised the essential material of the Forest is water. Spongy, wet humus surface – becoming firmer in the Spring as trees suck up the water. Plan a combination of running water and wood. After a long search find a water source and two fallen trees lying down slope. Diverted the water along branch troughs, through the roots of a fallen sycamore down its trunk, off along more troughs to finally pour over a stone and disappear into the ground."

David Nash
Wooden Waterway 1978

"My aim is to present people with something that seems to 'belong', yet which is outside their normal experience. This can by-pass some of the prejudice experienced when people are confronted by something that tells them it is art – clearing the way for a more open response."

Richard Harris
Cliff Structure 1978

"The construction system used in ***Quarry Structure*** was originally conceived as a bridging device to follow the line of a stream. Unexpectedly I found the quarry site which immediately made sense of the idea. The quarry had been fenced off, overgrown and forgotten. The structure, nosing out into the path, acts as a device to open up the space, both physically and visually."

Richard Harris
Quarry Structure 1978

“The sculptures I have sited at Grizedale are intended to appeal more to the senses than the intellect, and those with little knowledge of modern art will be able to ‘understand’ them if they approach with an open mind . . . The sculptures are abstract and have no reference to the figurative subjects. I make abstract art because since around 1920 the best contemporary art has been abstract.”

David Evison
Untitled 1980

"My work has been strongly influenced by the character and nature of wood and I work by carving and constructing elements within the structure. A mixture of building up and carving means changes in order and emphasis and allows the form a period of evolution and synthesis of differing images.

The Forest was full of rabbits, so to make a giant rabbit seemed a good starting point . . . I wanted a friendly image to come across and one that could simply be enjoyed. I feel this was achieved because after a few weeks the site had turned into a popular picnic place, with children climbing over the sculpture."

Alan Grimwood
Rabbit 1980

"The Birdman's Hut is a future relic. The birdman has flown away. The remains of his earthly abode are decaying, but still reminiscent of his erstwhile magic. In the future's future, we are confronted with the remainders of post-technological shamanism. Birds now inhabit the hut. Nature gently takes over the old place of power. They blend together as the seasons go by and will, sometime, be one again."

David Kemp
Scale Green Birdman – or – Departure Lounge 1981

"It involved, at the time of working within the forest, a fundamental challenge to working method and responses . . . Perhaps the real legacy is not the temporary or permanent external evidence sited at some point in the landscape, but the inner resource which has to be found in some acutely specific way at the time."

Paul Mason
Up One Two Three 1981

"I was taken by the image of the hunter stalking his prey, the mutual transmutation that would occur. The ***Deer Hunter*** is the effigy of the prey becoming the hunter or the hunter becoming the prey. It stands hidden amongst deciduous trees, his body is perfectly camouflaged. In a frozen stance, he waits . . ."

David Kemp
Deer Hunter 1982

"I became interested in the idea of objects emitting inaudible sounds that varied with their shape and size. ***Ting*** was conceived for Grizedale in this sense. A pure shape (40 feet diameter steel circle) tightly woven through the branches of a tree, that could not be seen in total, only sensed; and existing within the magnitude of organic forms offered by the forest. A silence within a noise."

Colin Rose
Ting 1983

"I felt as though all my senses were becoming much more attuned to the forest environment working outside every day one became accustomed for seeing and hearing things which I am sure most walkers passing through wouldn't notice. My sense of hearing 'opened' out, the squeaks and screech of birds and buzzards wheeling on the thermals overhead never ceased to amaze me. This 'opening out' of my senses also affected my work. I hope it became much more subtle, less brash, more in keeping with the forest."

Nigel Lloyd
Stone Red Wallow 1983

"Having come from a large town to live in Grizedale, I noticed a sharpening of senses that had dulled. Instead of closing off noise, and any distracting forms, as I do in the city, I felt more inquisitive . . . The place was complete. Important elements of wind, night, darkness and all changes of weather and their effects in transforming natural form were abundant and very potent . . . the sculptures were titled as watchers or observers of their particular forest region."

Ken Turnell
The Eye 1984

"**Forest Fugue** is situated in one of the long aisles, made by timber thinning operations in a spruce plantation. The aisle is reminiscent of a cathedral (or maybe cathedrals are reminiscent of trees). The sculpture represents an organ, and plays a silent requiem for the stumps."

David Kemp
Forest Fugue 1984

"The idea of a maze pattern seemed to be appropriate, as one invariably gets lost in the forest, and it has connections with the cup and ring marks at home, it also reads as a mandala, so that several correlated ideas exist at the same time and can be read and interpreted individually by the viewer. The drawing is let into the stone in line and as broken surfaces, the light catches them in different ways and the symmetry of the pattern is broken when the rock surface rolls back to give a feeling of being there and not being there."

Gilbert Ward
Celtic Ring 1984

"In making the spires I wanted to concentrate the feelings I get from within a pine wood of an almost desperate growth and energy driving upward. The spire also seemed appropriate with its references to churches and, in particular, the Cathedral with its architectural use of lines leading the eye skyward. I also felt a similarity in the subdued brown light and stillness found both in cathedrals and pine forests."

Andy Goldsworthy
Seven Spires 1984

"There is a small area of public sculpture I am interested in. A sculpture which is not limiting, 'ideal', or just dumping the sculptor's badge on the community: an intimate relationship between the sculptor, the community and the environment. A sculpture which does not increase the alienation between art and the public but creates as many paradoxes and dimensions as possible within the context of the work. The work should be of its time and place. It should talk to the people because the problems it deals with are the very same ones that the people deal with and see every day."

Michael Winstone
Midnight Feast 1984

"The materials blend in well with the outcrops and trees. The lines are massive and strong, and the craftsmanship (a miniature drystone walling technique) is superb and has received the admiration of hard-bitten local farmers. But, above all, the subject has captured the imagination of the children . . ."

Gerald Pinder, Headmaster
Satterthwaite & Rusland School

Donald Rankin
The Fort 1984

"Whilst at Grizedale I became more aware of the importance of the process of making sculpture . . . The sculpture is the final form that people see of my activities but it is only the residue of the story of my relationship with the landscape and the people. The sculpture was not primarily conceived of as a tree of polarities, infinity, growth – life itself on a basic level . . . I liked the paradox between the growing plantation of trees having just started their life and the reconstructured tree which was recycled – a reincarnation from a single old oak tree that had been felled."

Helena Stylianides
Tree Sculpture 1984

"Archaeology is a science. Art is not.
in his 'archaeology,' there is no need
entifically. The objects I make may ref
they are scientific remains. Time is an
work. An anecdote is given but the cho
– clay, wood, soil, grass, and stones –
change in the open air. After the work
control.

A preserved dry stone wall is alm
growing forest. I trapped and made
of the wall in a cage made of black-tarr
gives the wall a special meaning and s
and wall were combined into a new im

"The Ancient Forester, a figure of great antiquity, lurks deep in the Gothic forests and wilderness between our ears. From Cernunnos, the horned Celtic deity to Tolkien's Tom Bombardil, he represents an idealised image of man the hunter, the mystic, the guardian. He lives in responsible husbandry with nature, and seeks a symbiotic relationship with his environment and its renewable resources.

Centrally-heated, carpeted, cocooned and double-glazed, we are becoming separate from our real life-support systems. Dazzled by the power of our clever machines, we are sawing off the branch we sit on. **The Ancient Forester** is a noble ideal. The wooden figure is huge joke. It didn't cost an arm and a leg to make – only an oak tree. Timber!'

David Kemp
The Ancient Forester 1988

"After Alan Grimwood died I came to restore his ***Figure in a Pond*** and to build a 'monument' to him.

In making a 'monument' for Alan I looked back and find I have made a circus, unintentionally disturbing the peace of his figure already reigning over the pond . . . I hope he is enjoying the spectacle!"

"From the forest track the Sitka spruce seems to be a solid barrier. In the forest it is dark, quiet and carpeted with pine needles. ***Hollow Spruce*** acts as a filter through which to re-explore the light, sound, colour and space of the dense spruce."

Richard Harris
Hollow Spruce 1989

"When I arrived at Grizedale in April, it looked like a forest in the northern mountain area of Japan where I was born. But after a month I found Grizedale was entirely different.

I liked to walk through the Grizedale Forest with a compass in my pocket. When I came to a viewpoint, I took my compass and map out of my pocket. To feel the orientation in the forest is to feel the earth. At this stage of our civilization it is important to feel the earth. I am not pessimistic about the future of the human race. But the earth is the only one and it is difficult for us to live without it."

Masao Ueno – Japan
Axis of Earth 1990

"We can drive faster than a cheetah runs and kill quicker than a lion. We know how a horse moves and how a bird flies. We may be amazed by 'Wildlife on One,' but we forget, we do not live beside animals any more. Our admiration and the mystery of animals has been belittled by our achievement. We are not listening. They have senses and a reality that we have lost or never had."

Sally Matthews
A Cry in the Wilderness 1990

Petre Nikoloski – Yugoslavia
Living Space 1990

"The law of nature; the dry stone walls meeting the pine woods, silence, unpredictability deer, birds, wind, rain . . . Following the law of nature I built a wall. Enclosed a space; wall-home-house, warmth-womb-mother-woman, and all energy that exist inside that form. A wall – a desire to acknowledge the basic need to build, to change."

The Gallery

As part of the ongoing development of arts facilities within the forest, in 1987 the Grizedale Society took on the lease from the Forestry Commission of an old, redundant sawmill. The intention at the time was to demolish it to make way for another 10 car parking spaces but it was saved and restored with cash raised from various trusts and foundations.

The gallery was designed to serve a didactic purpose: to complement the sculptures within the forest itself and to introduce the public to some of the ideas behind Grizedale. On display are maquettes, working drawings and three-dimensional work relating to activities which are or have been going on outside and which, hopefully, will lead the visitor on to the sculptures themselves. There is also an exhibition of wood-related crafts.

Inside the Gallery at Grizedale

Craftsmen & Painters in Residence

It proved possible to build a crafts workshop just behind the Gallery. This was equipped with woodworking machinery. The first craftsman-in-residence moved in in September 1989.

In 1990, it was decided to develop the attic space above the gallery into a studio for use by resident painters producing contemporary work.

Above: One of the first artists in residence, Joanna Hart, in the painting studio, 1991.

Left: Jonathan Stockton, craftsman in residence at Grizedale.

Right: David Carter, the first artist in residence, in the painting studio.

Grizedale takes art into the community. Pupils of Coniston Primary School worked with sculptor Chris Campbell to create this mammoth from elm cut-offs (1985).

Artist in schools project in action with sculptor Keith Alexander and Colin Wilbourne at Satterthwaite Primary School.

Woodland Management at Grizedale

The management of woodland at Grizedale has a considerable history. The forest which today provides enjoyment and inspiration for so many people owes its existence and prosperity directly to its use and economic importance for the production of timber and other woodland products over at least 850 years. Economic activity has sustained the woodlands and ensured that successive owners have maintained and expanded their area when over so much of the country the process has been of clearance and decline.

This traditional management began after the Norman Conquest when much of the land in Furness was granted to the monks of Furness Abbey. It has continued ever since.

Management was by "coppice with standards." The coppice was cut in regular cycles to provide the small wood needed, for example, for charcoal, whilst the "standards" of single stemmed trees were used for larger dimension timber required for construction and shipbuilding.

The value of coppice woodlands reached a peak in about 1860 with the rising demand by competing industries such as iron smelting, gunpowder works, and the many bobbin mills which supplied the thriving cotton industry in Lancashire. Thereafter, there was a rapid decline in demand until at the end of the 19th century the value of coppice woodland had dropped to a mere £6 per acre. This was when regular coppicing of the area around Grizedale ceased.

Since then these attractive broadleaved woodlands have been converted to "high forest" with single stems being grown on as "standards". These woodlands are now managed, principally, for their amenity value and for ecological and historical considerations.

Successive owners of Grizedale have all been involved with woodland management in one form or another which has resulted in the retention of these historically important broadleaved areas. Most notable among previous owners since the early 18th century were the families of Ford Ainslie and, latterly Brocklebank.

Richard Ford of Monk Coniston, ironmaster and founder of the Newland Iron Company, built Ford Lodge at Grizedale. Together with his son William and his granddaughter Agnes, he was responsible for planting large numbers of oak and ash trees on rough pasture land, with the objective of producing valuable coppice for timber production.

Agnes was a great beauty and she married Henry Ainslie, a doctor practising in Kendal. Their son Montague, with the continuing family interests in the iron industry, built a new hall on the site of Ford Lodge and became a major benefactor to the locality. He also planted one and a half million European Larch trees in the Grizedale woodlands to provide long pitprops for his mines. Numbers of these trees can still be seen.

In 1903, the estate was sold to Harold Brocklebank who invested at Grizedale considerable sums of money derived from his interests in the Cunard Shipping Co. All of the Ainslie buildings were pulled down and a new Hall and a whole series of estate buildings was created. With the exception of the Hall which was subsequently demolished, these buildings have given a unique opportunity through sensitive adaptation to create the forestry and arts complex of today.

Brocklebank was a keen sportsman and a great tree planter. He planted

Skidding tractor at the roadside in the Forest. The felled poles in the picture have been pulled to the roadside for the crosscutter to convert into sawlogs and woodpulp

many woodlands using Douglas fir, Japanese larch, Norway and Sitka spruce and Scots pine and gave names such as "China" and "New South Wales" to the plantations, which survive to the present time and evoke memories of the distant locations to which ships of the Cunard line sailed. Harold Brocklebank died in 1936 and it was his wish that the estate should be sold in one lot.

When the Forestry Commission acquired the Grizedale Hall Estate in 1936 it consisted of 2962 acres of agricultural land, 1067 acres of ancient woodland and plantations, a mansion, a country house, seven farm houses and 36 other houses and cottages, complete with tenants, and, even a fire engine!

From 1937 until the outbreak of war in 1939 the upper slopes of degraded sheepgrazings were planted mostly with Larch, Spruce and Pine until the needs of war changed the emphasis from planting to harvesting of timber. Timber production and sawmilling proceeded apace using the skills of the Timber Corps and a battalion of Land Army Girls. Fortunately some woodlands were spared – particularly the oak woodlands and the policy woodlands around the Hall.

The Hall found new use as a POW compound for German Officers. Despite the wooden watchtowers and night-time floodlighting, the escape attempts of prisoners provided regular excitement – most famous of all being von Werra – known as "The One That Got Away" following his later successful attempt to escape. Sadly, the dilapidation of the Hall during army occupation, the high cost of repair and the lack of a tenant conspired to result in the demolition of the building in 1957.

The post-war planting programme gained added momentum. The woodlands felled during the War had to be replanted and there was continued expansion of the forest by planting on the poorer hill grazings. When this work was completed, 75 per cent of the former agricultural land had been transformed to forest but by maintaining and concentrating farming on the better sites, the production from agriculture was undiminished.

Labour was required for planting and a force of 70 were employed in 1948, half being transported daily from Barrow but an increasing number being accommodated in houses newly-built in the valley. Road construction in the forest began in 1948 as unemployment relief work for up to 35 men. The timber was pulled from the forest by horses so the roads had to be closely spaced. As tractors, equipped with winches and later forwarders with cranes and trailers have taken over, many of these early roads have been abandoned and now provide attractive walks and recreational routes.

The establishment of the forest road system allowed access for timber production from the new forest areas and these new woodlands began to show an economic return. Special attention was directed to managing the attractive broadleaved mixed woodlands which had been retained on the lower more fertile slopes of the valley and this will ensure their place in the landscape for future generations.

The evolution of the forest took on a new and exciting turn at the start of the 1960s. This was to experiment with new roles for the forest to include the integration of forest management, wildlife management and the recreational use of the forest by the public.

The vital extra ingredient to achieve success with this new approach was inspired by forward thinking forest managers such as Jack Chard, conservation of forests, and Bill Grant, head forester at Grizedale, who ably fulfilled this role. From 1960 onwards a model outdoor recreational plan has been developed at Grizedale which has pioneered the responsible use of forests by the public. This plan continues to be refined and developed. The facilities at Grizedale have brought enjoyment and pleasure to many thousands of visitors and local people through a variety of educational opportunities and natural history interests.

The establishment of the Grizedale Society, an autonomous Charitable Trust, and its Theatre-in-the-Forest added the arts to Grizedale's growing repertoire of interests, and what better surroundings could be found for the performance of drama, music and dance? Later came the Sculpture Project, again built on the foundation of the working forest with all the pieces "site-related".

There are two essential features which have guided the hands of all those involved in the developments at Grizedale. The first is that it has always been, and remains, a working forest with the production of timber its main activity and by far the largest generator of income. In excess of 20000 tonnes of mainly softwood timber are now harvested each year for use in sawmills throughout Wales, the North of England and South Scotland; in carton board manufacture at Workington; and for chipboard production at Hexham. Up to 50 Forestry Commission staff and contractors are engaged on this work and in the replanting and management of the young trees that follows. These activities provide the backbone of the forest, on which all other activities are based.

The second essential feature is quality. Everything must be to the highest standard of quality and service. Easy to aspire to but difficult to attain, all facilities should be constructed and maintained to achieve this objective. This is most evident in the design of the buildings which form the Grizedale centre, but it must also reach each picnic site and trail and the planning of every forest operation.

The 1980s saw the maturity of the oldest of the Forestry Commission's planted woodlands. The generally even-aged blocks of plantation could now be broken up and the forest redesigned by careful planning and timing of felling and replanting. The local foresters, working with landscape architects, devised a Landscape Plan which guides the progress of felling and restocking. The aim is to have each age class from the youngest to the oldest trees present throughout the whole forest. This is achieved by leaving 5 to 10 years between the felling of adjoining blocks. Each felling area or "coupe" is designed to be of a size and shape which fits into the landscape and accommodates the conservation and management of wildlife. A proportion of trees, such as the Douglas fir and Norway spruce above the Grizedale Centre are retained to a greater age than would normally be considered economic owing to their beauty and strategic location in the landscape.

The redesign of the forest has allowed the introduction, when restocking, of a network of broadleaved trees and open space as corridors following the forest's many water courses. In time, these will become important for the movement and habitation of wildlife as well as linking the landscapes of the valley and upper slopes and providing windfirm edges and stability for future timber crops.

Fences are erected around all of the replanted areas. These are essential in order to exclude the deer who would otherwise browse the young trees and severely limit their growth. The flowers and plants of the forest rapidly re-establish in the absence of grazing. Experiments are being conducted to determine when it will be safe to remove these fences.

Wildlife and recreational developments have also continued during the 1980s. The clearance of *Rhododendron ponticum* which was choking the ground vegetation in many of the Valley oakwoods has been undertaken and is now virtually complete. Many of the original dams and tarns have been refurbished to maintain their value to wildlife.

The Visitor Centre complex was redesigned from scratch to result in the award winning complex of buildings where visitors can now find all the information they need on wildlife, recreation, the arts and the timber production which sustains the forest. The status of the forest was confirmed by its designation as a "Forest Park" in 1987.

Where does this leave the foresters of Grizedale in the early 1990s? They can marvel at the achievements of the past and take pride from the fact that Grizedale now stands as a model for the multiple purpose forest where industry is provided with timber, the public are welcomed and wildlife is sensitively conserved and managed. This provides the basis of modern forest planning throughout the nation.

The forest however does not stand still. A regular cycle of timber harvesting has been entered: trees will be felled as the Landscape Plan dictates; and the cleared areas replanted new views will be opened up; further opportunities for conservation and recreation will be presented. How much further should the forest managers go in pursuing new developments? Perhaps it is a time to take stock of what we have, to ensure that the objective of quality is being met and to consider how the balance between the many uses of forest can be best maintained for the advantage of all. Surprises will be in store. The forester may plan, but he cannot predict, for example, the effect of the gales which in February 1990 blew down an entire year's harvesting programme in the space of a couple of days. It is the ability to respond to such events, to balance the many activities now represented in the forest and to use the programme of felling and restocking to redesign the forest for the next generation that provide today's challenges.

Brian Mahony

with acknowledgements to
Mr J S R Chard
Mr J C Voysey
from whose writings much of the
historical information is drawn.

Brian Mahony is the Forestry Commission's Forest District Manager for South Lakes Forest District.

Opposite: Grizedale is an excellent example of the integration of farming and forestry.

Red stag at dusk

Red deer hinds, Grizedale

Wildlife of the Forest

Forests provide sanctuaries for wild life. When uneconomic hill farms are afforested a dynamic successional process comes into play. As the ubiquitous sheep are excluded, grass and heather grow rank. Voles multiply and foxes, weasels, kestrels and short-eared owls come in to prey upon them. The true moorland birds are gradually phased out, and as the young trees grow clear of the vegetation, roe deer establish themselves, and there may be a temporary influx of whinchats on the drier sites and of reed buntings on the more fertile. Then willow warblers appear, meadow pipits give place to tree pipits, and as the crop closes towards thicket we usually have redpolls and the first chaffinches. The vole population collapses, and the only bird to persist right through from moorland to high forest is the tiny wren. Harriers appear from time to time when the pre-thicket bird population is at its peak, and they also may take voles.

While the local pattern can vary dramatically from year to year, sustained planting programmes provide a constant succession of fresh habitats, so that taken overall most species at this stage of the forest's development are changing their ground rather than varying their numbers.

Once thicket is formed we have a different situation and are concerned with a much slower and usually quite undramatic build-up of the true forest community. Moreover, we can no longer assess this by sitting on some hilltop and scanning wide stretches of country through binoculars. Apart from casual encounters, no one can expect to see wildlife in dense evergreen forest without putting in a lot of hard work, or else, as at Grizedale, first having it done for him. Successful observation depends upon placing oneself in the right spot at the right time and in the right manner. This involves first of all acquiring an intimate knowledge of the topography, and then making frequent reconnaissances at dusk and dawn and at key periods of the year – particularly those when song or courtship display or rutting activity is anticipated. In the case of mammals it also involves taking every possible opportunity to track them during snow.

It is perhaps not generally realised that even in a fully planted forest as much as one tenth of the area is left for rides and road alignments. If there are also large watercourses, deep gullies, rock outcrops, peat hags of other sorts of ground uneconomic to cultivate, the proportion actually without trees will be even greater. Changes in the character of the vegetation and its associated insect life which were started by the removal of sheep grazing continue in these rides and openings, and aided now by shelter, progressively diversify them as food sources. At the same time, however uniform it may have seemed to start with, the surrounding crop is itself influenced by variable site factors, and will begin to exhibit local differences in height and vigour which at this stage of growth are often quite pronounced. The combination of these two trends brings further complexity to the pattern of wildlife distribution, and in our present state of knowledge, makes it somewhat risky to generalise on its development.

One fairly safe assumption is that the only mammal which both feeds and breeds in the bare floor of the thicket stage plantation is the mole, and the only bird to do so is the woodcock. Both utilise the more fertile sites where decomposition of the suppressed vegetation is promoted by earthworms. Elsewhere the decaying peat supports splendid displays of colourful fungi. Perhaps the only bird to become both generally distributed and numerous throughout this period is the chaffinch. Towards the end of it wood pigeons start to nest socially on warm south-facing slopes or towards the edges of the forest, and there is a big influx of them when the bilberries are ripe. Many species feed or hunt along the rides but breed elsewhere, and before its recent general decline the most typical raptor was the barn owl. The main contrast with moorland or pre-thicket conditions is that although fewer kinds of bird may breed, the establishment of shelter encourages a greater variety and much larger numbers either to stay on over winter or come in specially to roost.

Roe deer reach peak numbers in the pre-thicket plantations but when canopy closes the population collapses. Red deer find sanctuary in the dense cover of thicket stage crops and move out from them to feed. Their numbers continue to rise as the trees get older. At Grizedale we have some of the only truly indigenous woodland red deer in Britain; elsewhere they belong to the hills or are descended from introductions.

Before the pole stage is reached roads are constructed to bring out the produce of the first thinnings, and these make a further and far-reaching contribution to the diversity of the forest habitat. Bare earth, rock and gravel are exposed in borrow pits and quarries, and in-fill and side-cut along the verges. In terrain so largely smothered by peat these exposures add greatly to fertility, which is also enhanced by the frequent use of whinstone and limestone for road metal, and the dust and splashes of passing traffic. This traffic assists dispersal and colonisation by many new plants. Foxglove is typical but the most intriguing alien of our forest roads is probably the tiny New Zealand willow herb. Slugs thrive in less acid conditions, and local snail colonies are established which attract the song thrush. Hedgehogs are enticed into places where they were previously unknown, and scrapes of bare earth and a fresh sward encourage the exploring rabbit. In Grizedale we have some 70 miles of roads.

Although for economic reasons it is not done so intensively as in the past, thinning is preceded by "brashing", in which some of the dead lower branches are cut away to give access for inspection and marking. Brashing like digging, seems always to be accompanied by the robin. It also reveals the old nests of many unsuspected residents in previous years. Surveys in plantations of mixed species have shown that Sitka spruce is a preferred choice for nest building, the angle and interval of branching, stiffness of twigs, and density of foliage being apparently ideal. The discoveries on one occasion included a complete heronry.

The first thinning is usually done about 20 years after planting, and this operation is then repeated at roughly five-year intervals until the crop reaches its economic optimum – but of course not its physical maturity – at around 50 years of age. These periods will vary according to local rates of growth and the requirements of the market. The effect of each thinning is to space the remaining trees wider apart, let in more light and warmth to the forest floor, and leave behind a debris of lop and top and cut over stumps, all of which are factors beneficial to wild life. Movement becomes less hindered and views are progressively extended. The rotting branch wood gives ground cover and decaying stumps make nest holes. Mosses and ferns begin to establish themselves and an expanding invertebrate fauna colonises the needle litter. Shrews increase and the ground nesting coat tit is added to wren and robin. The trees themselves harbour a more numerous and varied insect life, helped as they grow older by lichen-encrusted twigs and the rough flaking of the bark on their lower boles. Roving flocks of mixed tits, tree creepers, goldcrests and other birds become a regular feature of the winter woods, and often lead one to a roosting owl.

The barn owl moves on before the trees begin to overhang the rides, and although tawny owls are more often heard, its immediate successor is probably the long-eared, whose pellets show that it too feeds on voles, and sometimes finches. The long-eared owl will nest on the ground in newly-thinned pole crops, whereas the tawny usually waits to take over the nest of crow or sparrowhawk. Like the sparrowhawk, the tawny owl hunts between the trees, and its pellets contain a high proportion of shrews, and later on of wood mice.

The woodmouse population only builds up after the trees have begun to set seed, and as it was presumably absent from large areas of the original moorland and as the first cone crops are erratic, its distribution is often very localised. The pips and stones voided in bird roosts help to keep it going. After the first heavy seed year it spreads more widely and then declines again as the supply gives out. The red squirrel follows a similar pattern but can travel over much greater distances and one is often surprised to discover from a litter of stripped cones that it has recently arrived in some remote corner of the forest, apparently from nowhere.

Roebuck, Grizedale Forest

We do not yet know how far Sitka spruce can support a permanent population of red squirrels. On its natural host, the Scots pine, the cones take two years to ripen, and so some are always available. With Sitka spruce, even though scattered individuals will cone out of phase with the remainder, and older trees will have at least some cones annually, there is always a gap between the main fall of seed and the ripening of the next crop. In times of abundance the squirrels throw down large numbers of cones unopened, and if they can later retrieve them before the mice get to work this may possibly help to tide them over. One now finds siskins and crossbills working in Sitka spruce. Chaffinches and other birds catch a lot of seed in the air, and with siskins find it on the ground as well.

The ragged openings cause by windblow provide yet another type of wildlife habitat, which is perhaps more productive than any that went before. When the produce has been cleared the bare needle litter and the tangle of lop and top and upturned root plates is at first free of weed growth and the forester tries to get the ground replanted as soon as possible. If windblow coincides with a good seed year there may also be quite a lot of natural regeneration, and this is often supplemented by wind-borne sallow and birch, and sometimes alder. Rowan springs up freely from bird-carried seed which has been lying dormant on the forest floor. Needle litter is an ideal seed bed, and as it begins to decompose it releases nutrients and brings on a strong flush of grass and herbage. Roe deer find these warm sheltered clearings ideal and browse them heavily but, as usual, selectively. Broadleaves suffer the most damage, and relatively few of them are able to compete effectively with the planted crop. Voles recover and birds from earlier stages of the succession return temporarily until the trees again close thicket. The cycle repeats itself but always more richly than before, and the influence of the edge effect in increasing this variety is well known.

These windblow clearings give a foretaste of how the whole forest will develop now that rotation felling has begun. Although the first planting is carried out in large blocks it does not necessarily follow that harvesting will be done in the same manner. Thus the rate of growth varies from place to place, while the need to maintain regular supplies to established markets and to smooth out peak demands for labour and machinery requires the work to be spread over a longer period than before. Continuity of working implies cutting the same volume and therefore roughly the same area annually and this objective of sustained yield, one of the basic principles of forest management, requires the eventual establishment of a full succession of age classes. A second principle is ot conserve the forest environment which has taken so long to build up, and traditionally this involves arranging the size, shape and distribution of the annual felling coupes in such a way as to retain shelter until the new crop is established. In a situation where felling may always precipitate windblow, and in which the progress of mechanisation constantly demands larger areas for bigger machines, there are some arguments for modifying this concept. We lack experience to see the final picture, which involves landscaping as well as other considerations, but in my personal judgment it is the irregularities of the site that should be our guide. Selected remnants of windblown plantations and well placed groups of trees which have already withstood the gales and shown themselves windfirm need to be grown on to temper the blast for their neighbours and successors. These will diversify the landscape, and ensure that the complex wild